Raising Great Kids

by Joyce Robitaille

*Special thanks
to Allison and Drew
for permission to use their picture.*

"Raising Great Kids"
is a revision of my book
"Raising Well-Behaved Kids – A SIMPLE GUIDE"

YOU ARE YOUR CHILD'S MOST IMPORTANT TEACHER

When it comes to physical safety, we automatically teach our children not to put their finger in an electric outlet, not to touch something that is hot and to look both ways before crossing the street.

We need to be as diligent when it comes to teaching them what kind of behavior is acceptable and what isn't.

Children learn from the behavior and actions of those around them.
It is your responsibility to love, guide and set an example for your child.

Being a parent is the biggest responsibility you will ever have, but it can also be the most rewarding experience as you become your child's most important teacher.

Contents

WHAT IS DISCIPLINE?

Discipline is teaching a child what is acceptable behavior and what isn't.

And . . . teaching a child that there are consequences when he/she does not behave in an acceptable manner.

With positive discipline, you can help your child develop confidence, self-control, respect for others and a sense of responsibility. These are qualities they will need to be resourceful, self-sufficient, independent and content adults.

RULES

Children need rules. Though they may complain and fight against rules, deep down they want them. It gives them a sense of stability. They know what is expected of them without having to guess or push you to see what the limits are. They need to *know* what those limits are.

Every household and family is unique and has their own rules. Rules help to maintain order and stability. **The younger the child is when the rules are in place, the better.**

Here are some rules to consider:
- **Limits** on time spent watching TV, on the computer, cell phone and other electronics. *See the chapter: "Time for Themselves".*
- **Chores must be completed.**
  Expect chores to be done in a timely manner --- NOT when the child "feels like it."

- **Everyone eats dinner together.**
  (At the table, not in front of the TV)
  *Dinner time is a time for the family
  to come together and share their day.
  Agree to cell phones off while eating.*
- **Have set bed times** *Children should
  have a consistent bed time. Set times
  that are appropriate for their age. If
  child is not sleepy, you may allow him
  to read quietly in bed until he is.*
- **Set curfews** for older children.
- **Children should always let their
  parents know where they are** and call
  if they are going to be late getting
  home.

Some rules (like bed times and dinner
together) may occasionally be broken because
of circumstances.

Some rules have *no* exceptions (like a child
letting her parents know where she is).

Having rules in place helps avoid arguments
later. You must also **be consistent** in
enforcing these rules. Every day shouldn't be
a game of "Let's make a Deal"!

Example: Anna spends hours every evening on her cell phone texting and checking face-book. You yell at her:

"Don't you have anything better to do? Get off that phone!"

If some days you get upset with her about something and other days you don't, you are sending mixed messages. How do you expect her to be cooperative?

It is best to already have rules in place, like how much time is allowed on TV, phones, etc. And to stick to those rules. Children need to clearly understand what the rules are and what is expected of them.

Now you can say, "Anna, you know the rule. You're allowed an hour after school on electronics and another ½ hour after dinner if your homework is done. Turn it off."

Have consequences for breaking the rules, trying to match the consequence with the rule broken.

In this case, you would take Anna's cell phone away for the rest of the day. If she breaks the rule again, she'd lose use of her phone for longer.

Or: The babysitter tells you that Johnny spent the whole day watching TV. Johnny knows the rule is only 2 hours. A reasonable consequence may be NO TV for a week.

NOTE:

It is never too late to make a new rule. Let your child know that you've thought about the situation and you have decided a rule is needed.

Make a list of the rules you already have and new ones you might like to add.

RESPONSIBILITY AT HOME

Children need jobs around the house. This teaches them responsibility.

A toddler can help return his toys to the proper place when play time is over.
Older ones can clear the table, fold towels, fill the dishwasher, vacuum, mow the lawn.

Sometimes breaking down a chore into manageable parts will help your child succeed. For example, simply telling a young child to clean the playroom can be overwhelming. Ask her to do one thing at a time, then go on to the next.

1. Put the blocks away.
2. Put the cars in their case.
3. Put the crayons in the box.
4. Stack the books on the table.

If there is more than one child, give each one a different thing to do.

Telling a child (even an older child) to clean his room can also be overwhelming. Again, break it into parts, requesting one thing at a time:

1. Pick up and put your dirty clothes in the hamper.
2. Throw away paper and garbage hanging around.
3. Sort through that pile of papers.
4. Put your books in the bookcase.

And so forth.

Show appreciation for a job well done. When chores are *not* done, take away a privilege.

Every child is different, so choose consequences that suit the child.

For example, withholding allowance may work well for the child who values his money. For the social child, no playtime with friends may be a better consequence.

Write up a Chore Chart and post it on the refrigerator. Have your children check off their chores after they have done them.

CONSEQUENCES VERSUS PUNISHMENT

Think in terms of consequences, rather than punishments.

A consequence is directly related to a child breaking a rule or misbehaving and is a way of teaching your child a lesson in a positive way.

A punishment, on the other hand is often done in anger and is intended to hurt or demean a child, either mentally or physically. It is negative approach that can cause a child to feel unworthy and angry.

Think of times when you may have used a negative approach when disciplining. How can you do it differently next time?

FOLLOWING THROUGH!

If your child is whining and making demands, do you give in or do you take the time to teach him that his behavior is unacceptable. Do you show him that there are consequences for bad behavior?

Example: You stop at pharmacy on the way to the movies.   Jimmy begs for a toy at the checkout. You tell him "no", but he begs even more and starts to cry. You tell him if he doesn't stop right now he will not go to the movies.

He continues to beg and scream. You are embarrassed by his behavior and want to give in simply to quiet him down.

1. Do you give in and buy him the toy because you are tired of hearing him?

2. Or do you NOT buy him the toy and NOT take him to the movies?

If you make threats and don't follow through, you are teaching your child that you do not mean what you say. Your child learns that HE is in control. That HE can get his way by being noisy and obnoxious.

Remember: **Children NEED parameters and WANT to know what is expected of them.**

Lower yourself to your child's level, look directly into his eyes and (without yelling) tell him you will not tolerate this type of behavior. And don't!

NEVER REWARD BAD BEHAVIOR!

Do NOT take him to the movies. If there are other siblings involved, you may feel it is not fair to them. However, by not going to the movies, all the children are learning a lesson. They will all learn that you are serious AND they will think twice about repeating that type of behavior.

Following through is one of the most important rules for disciplining a child effectively!

You are teaching your child what is acceptable behavior and that there are consequences for bad behavior. It is *your* responsibility to teach your child. **You cannot expect him to be well-behaved if you don't take the time to teach him!**

I know of a young father who took his children out for lunch. They were promised ice cream afterwards. But the children began bickering with each other. The father told them if they didn't behave, they would not get ice cream. The children continued to argue. The father did not repeat the threat. He ordered a hot-fudge sundae for himself and nothing for the children and proceeded to eat it in front of them.
Do you suppose his children ever misbehaved in a restaurant again?

Make an effort to follow-through when you discipline today. Think about how things have turned out when you DIDN'T.

GOOD MANNERS AND RESPECT

It is up to us to teach our children manners. Good manners show respect for others and their feelings.

Example: Jenny's grandmother offers her a piece of pumpkin pie.

Jenny sticks out her tongue and screams, "That's yucky."

Do you laugh or do you let Jenny know that she is being disrespectful and tell her to apologize?

Teach your child to say "No thank you" when offered something she doesn't want.

Example: Jimmy opens a birthday gift from Aunt Sara. It's a game. He doesn't like it so he pouts and says "What a stupid gift!"

Let Jimmy know that his reaction is rude and hurtful. Point out to him that his aunt bought the gift with the best intentions.   She was not aware that he doesn't like board games.

Teach your child to accept a gift with gratitude even if he doesn't like it.

If your child continues to react in a manner that is disrespectful, it should not be tolerated. Calmly tell your child what the consequence will be if they continue. THEN FOLLOW THROUGH.

Teach your child to say "please" and "thank you".   Children will do this without question when they see their parents do it, too.

Teach your children to acknowledge gifts. Example: If Jimmy receives a birthday card with money in it from Grandma, he should call Grandma and thank her.

Teach your child to respect older people. Example: If an older person enters a room where there are no available chairs and Jenny is sitting on one, teach her to stand and offer her chair to that person.

Teach your child not to interrupt you when you are talking to another adult. Unless it is an emergency (like he needs to use the potty or the house is on fire.)

Children learn manners and respect from their parents' example.

These are just a few examples.
What manners have you taught your children?

NO GUILT!

If your child asks for a new pair of sneakers because he wants the latest fashion, but his sneakers are still perfectly fine . . .

Don't let him put a guilt trip on you.
Because his best friend just got a pair is not a reason to get them.

Whether you are financially able or not . . .
don't give in to something simply because he wants it.

Just like the toddler who screams at the checkout for candy, if you give in, your child will try to wear you down every time she wants something.

Tell your child that your money is hard-earned and it will not be spent on something that is frivolous.

If your child *needs* new sneakers, tell her how much you are willing to spend and that she will have to earn and pay the difference if she wants a more expensive pair.

When they grow up they will quickly learn that in "real life", people do not get everything they want.

They need to realize that they must earn and work for the things they want.

An effective way to prevent yourself from giving in when your child is trying to wear you down, is to tell your child, "I need to think about it." And tell her you'll discuss it later. This gives you time to consider your reasons for saying "no" and how you want to answer.

Have you taken a "guilt trip" lately? Did you regret giving in? How could you have responded differently?

TRUST YOUR JUDGEMENT

Sometimes your child will ask to do something that you just don't feel comfortable about. If you can't come up with a reason other than that, it is okay to say to her:

"I'm not sure why, but I just don't feel comfortable with that."

If your child protests, don't back down. **Not feeling at ease about something is a good enough reason to say no.**

Believe it or not, sometimes that is exactly what your child *wants* you to say, even if he won't admit it.

When you make the decision *for* them it gets them off the hook. They can tell their friends, "My dad (or Mom) won't let me."

Example: Jenny's friends are going to see a horror movie.   Jenny doesn't like horror

21

movies. They scare her. She really doesn't want to go but is too embarrassed to say so. You don't feel it's a suitable movie. When you tell Jenny she can't go, she is relieved.

Example: Jimmy's new friend wants him to go to his house. Jimmy doesn't know him very well and is not sure he wants to.   But his friend has been pressuring him so Jimmy asks you if he can go.

You have never met this boy's family. You may have noticed that this boy has too much freedom to do whatever he wants. Or you just feel uneasy about it. You can simply tell Jimmy "No, I don't feel comfortable with you going there." Jimmy is off the hook and he can blame his parents.

Whether your child really *wants*
what she is asking for or not,
**if you feel uncomfortable with it,
go with your own better judgement.**

Think of an instance when allowing something that you are not comfortable with, could hurt your child?

WORKING WITH YOUR CHILD'S FEELINGS

Example: You take your young child to swimming lessons. He cries and says he doesn't want to. You insist he go in with the class. But he simply hangs onto the side of the pool refusing to take part.

When your child cries again the next day, you may wonder if you should force him to do this. But you feel it is important that your child know how to swim.

Suggestion: Lower yourself to eye level with your child and say calmly, "Jimmy, I know you don't want to take swimming lessons. You don't have to *like* the lessons, but do what your teacher tells you."
You may be surprised to find him cooperating with the teacher. Why?

Because you have acknowledged his feelings and given him permission to *not* enjoy the lessons.

Example: Every morning you find yourself arguing with Jenny about what she should wear to school. What she chooses is inappropriate and you insist she wear what you have chosen.   Jenny is angry that she can't wear what she wants.

Suggestion: Select two outfits you feel are appropriate and lay them on the bed. Allow Jenny to choose which one she'd like to wear. Even if neither outfit is something she would have chosen on her own, Jenny picks one to wear. Why?

Because you have acknowledged Jenny's desire to make her own decision concerning what she should wear. You have allowed her the opportunity to choose.

Acknowledging your child's feelings is important. It lets them know you care even if you don't give them exactly what they want.

Can you think of a time when working with your child's feelings helped the situation?

RESPONSIBILITY
FOR THEIR ACTIONS

If your child has misbehaved at school or while playing sports, an apology to a teacher or coach may be in order.

Example: You receive a note from school that Jimmy has been sending hateful text messages to a teacher or a classmate. They are able to show you evidence that your child did indeed send the texts.

DO NOT defend your child's bad behavior. There is *nothing* to be gained by doing so.

Teach your child to admit when he is wrong and to apologize when it is necessary. Give him consequences for his actions.

It is also your child's responsibility to take action to correct a mistake **even if not intentional.**

Example: Jimmy is playing with a ball and accidently throws it too far and breaks a neighbor's window.

If Jimmy did not do it on purpose, do not become angry with him. **Do teach him responsible action.** Take him to the neighbor and have him apologize.

Have Jimmy ask the neighbor how he can help pay for the damage. If the neighbor has insurance, Jimmy can offer to do some yard work as a way to pay for the inconvenience.

Example: Jenny is playing with a friend's toy and breaks it. If Jenny broke the toy purposely or because of recklessness, she should apologize and earn the money to replace the toy or offer her friend one of her own toys as a replacement. There must also be a consequence for her behavior.

If Jenny broke the toy accidently, she should still apologize and find a way to replace the toy or make amends.

HONESTY AND TRUST

Your child needs to learn the importance of honesty.

A child may lie to avoid the consequence of his behavior, or because he doesn't want his parents to be disappointed in him.

Let your child know that when he lies or does something deceitful, he loses your trust in him and that you may not believe him even when he is telling the truth.

If your child admits what she did, let her know there will still be a consequence, but that you appreciate her honesty.

If you want your child to be honest, you must set an example. Don't lie and do not ask your child to lie for you.

Show your child that you can be trusted and believed. Do not break promises. Do not cheat or deceive others.

Can you think of other ways
to teach your child honesty?
Why is it so important
to set an example?

RESPECT WITH WORDS AND ATTITUDES

Has your child caused another child hurt or embarrassment by gossiping about them? Has your child treated another child unkindly in any way?

Example: You hear Jenny talking with her friends about the new girl in their class. You hear them all laugh when one of them says, "She asked me if she could sit with us at lunch. I told her that we don't allow dummies at our table."

Ask Jenny and her friends how they would feel if someone treated them that way. Ask them: "What if you were the new girl in a school. Do you think it would be a little scary and lonely not knowing anyone? Would you want your classmates to make fun of you or would you want them to make you feel welcome?"

When Jenny's friends leave, tell her that even if she didn't make the hurtful comment, just by going along with her friends she was saying it was okay. This was just as bad and equally unkind.

Example: Jimmy is invited to join his friend's family when they go to the beach. Jimmy says to his brother, "Ha! I get to go to the beach. You don't."

Bragging should NEVER be tolerated. Children should learn that whatever it is they are bragging about does NOT make them any better than the other person. It can also be hurtful. The most effective way to teach Jimmy this lesson is by not allowing him to go to the beach.

Example: Your child criticizes another child's appearance, disabilities or religious beliefs. Let your child know that he should never judge other children because they are not like him. **Teach your child to respect the differences between himself and others.**

> How can you set an example of using speech that is beneficial to others instead of hurtful?

SELF-ESTEEM

High self-esteem comes from feeling good about yourself.

- **Love your child for who they are.**
Don't compare them to their siblings or friends. Don't tell them you wish they were more athletic like their brother or smarter like their friend.

- **Point out their strong points.**
Help them build on their strengths, instead of emphasizing their weaknesses.

- **Teach your child that what is important is: What kind of person she is inside**
Not what she owns, not how smart or how attractive she is.

While it's okay to tell your child that he or she looks nice occasionally, **don't put too much emphasis on looks.**

Don't always make a big deal about how pretty and adorable she is.
Otherwise, *she will believe that her worth is dependent on her looks.*

- **Praise your child when:**

Your child has worked hard at something.
Your child has behaved well.
Your child has done something nice for someone.

Don't shower your child with constant praise thinking it is what he needs to feel good about himself.   If the praise has no basis he will see through it.

- **Provide your child with ways in which he can help you.**

Feeling useful helps a child feel good about himself. Even when the job is quite simple, let them know you appreciate their help.

- **Build your children's self-esteem by teaching them to respect themselves.**

Example: Jenny wants to wear clothing that reveals too much. She may insist by saying "All the girls are wearing this, it's the style!"

Let her know dressing provocatively is not acceptable.   If you want what is best for her, **DO NOT BACK DOWN**. A young girl who is allowed to dress in clothing that reveals too much is not being taught to respect herself.

If your child "hates you" because you will not allow something that you know is not in her best interest, remember:
> **It is not necessary that your child always like you.**

> **All children need guidelines and limits. (whether they are 3 years old or 13) It is your responsibility to provide them.**

Someday they will appreciate your guidance.

Think about your own self-esteem. What makes you feel good about yourself? How can you nurture your child's self-esteem?

TIME FOR THEMSELVES

Every one of us needs time for ourselves. Cell phones and social media can be addictive. We feel we need to be "connected" every minute.

Our children are growing up believing they need to constantly check their phones and social media. They feel that they need to share their every thought and everything they do with their friends.

When a person's concept of themselves is based solely on the opinions of others, they don't develop the ability to discover who they truly are.

When they are bombarded with the opinions of people on social media, they don't learn how to think for themselves.

Children are not learning how to check in with themselves. Learning what brings them joy and purpose. Taking time to discover new hobbies. Getting to know yourself and feeling comfortable in your own space makes a person stronger and more confident.

To allow that to happen, a child needs time each day away from their cell phones, TV, video games and other electronics. They need quiet time to do more nurturing things.

Things you can do:
- Encourage your child to engage in creative things like art, woodworking, writing, knitting (yes people still do that) etc.
- Encourage reading. Begin by reading to your child. Visit the library with your child to look for books on subjects that interest him or her.
- Help your children discover the outdoors and nature. Bring them to the park to play or to nearby trails to walk.
- Support your child's interest in learning to play an instrument or playing sports. (check for financial resources, if you can't afford these things.)

Set an example. Take time away from social media. We ALL need "me" time.

- **Discipline with love.**

Discipline does not mean acting like a dictator. Using undue force and anger and making unreasonable demands will hurt your child, not help him.

A child needs a sense of security at home. This security comes when your child feels loved. Even as you discipline, **never withdraw your love from your child.**

- **Never belittle your child or make her feel unimportant.**

Discipline is meant to help your child, not hurt him. Remember the difference between consequence and punishment.

- **Sit with them and ask them about their day** (and listen).

- **Say "I love you" to your child every day.**

- **Spend time with your children.**
Do a craft project together. Go to the park.
Read to them. Play a board game. **Even busy parents can find a few minutes a day to devote some undivided attention to their child.**

- **If you are married, work to keep your relationship strong and loving. Don't fight in front of your kids.**
Nothing gives more security to a child than seeing his parents show respect and love to one another.

What do you do to help your child feel loved and secure?   Can you do more?

SETTING A GOOD EXAMPLE

Nothing teaches a child more effectively than setting a good example.

Respect: If you want your child to respect you, you must **show respect** for yourself and others.

Listen to your child. When your child speaks to you give him your attention. If you don't listen to your child, how can you expect your child to listen to you?

Set an example of being grateful. Express your appreciation for someone's help, food on the table, friends, family, a nice teacher. Talk about these things at dinner or when you tuck your child in at night. Learning to have a grateful attitude makes a child less wanting of things she doesn't have, by focusing on what she does have.

Set an example of a good attitude. Don't be a Blamer and a Complainer.

It is natural to be disappointed if something doesn't go your way. But a child will learn how to deal with the ups and downs of life much better if you teach your child that life doesn't always go the way we want. Blaming every one else for our misfortunes teaches our children not to take any responsibility for themselves. Complaining about everything and everyone teaches a child to look for the worst in people and situations instead of looking for the good.

**Teach your child:
It is not what HAPPENS to you,
but your ATTITUDE about what happens
that will determine how well you can
handle the bad stuff.**

Be the honest, responsible and
caring person that you want
your child to be.

TEENS

We tend to slide a bit when our kids become teenagers.   But they still need our guidance.

Everything discussed in the prior chapters is not only still important, but in many ways MORE important.

They still need:
> Rules
> Responsibility at Home
> Chores
> Manners
> Responsibility for their actions
> Respect for themselves and others

We still need to:
> Trust our Judgement
> Follow through
> Let them know we love them
> Listen to them
> Set a good example

It is only natural that our children will have more freedom the older they get. Sometimes we need to add new rules or adapt old ones to their age.

More important than ever, **they should always let you know where they are.** If they will be late getting home, call! If they miss curfews, repeatedly, have consequences --- like taking away car privileges if they have their license.

They shouldn't have friends over when you are not home. Unless, for example it is a best friend you are comfortable with.

You should know who their friends are. Insist you meet the kids they are hanging out with. Have them over.

Don't allow them to meet up with a gathering of teens at another home when there are no adults present. Make it a point to meet the parents of the kids your child spends time with. I have a friend whose son still remembers when he was a teen and going to a new friend's home for the first time. His mother accompanied him and brought a plant for the parents as a way to introduce herself. He was mortified at the time, but he survived!

Converse with your teen.
Show them you are interested in hearing about their day. If they seem unhappy, ask them what is bothering them. Listen to what they have to say without judging them. If they are receptive, give advice gently.
Tell them more about yourself. What challenges you've faced. What dreams you had as a teenager. Encourage them to talk about their own dreams. (Again, do not judge them.)

Let them know you love them.

DON'T STOP BEING A PARENT.
THEY NEED YOU MORE THAN EVER.

Take a moment to think about the last time you had a good conversation with your teen. How can you strengthen your relationship?

REMEMBER

YOU are the parent.

YOU are the person your
child looks to for guidance.

Set rules and limits.

Do not send mixed messages.
Follow through!

Be firm.
(without guilt)

Listen to your child.

Set a good example.

Discipline with love!

Comments are welcomed at:
raisingkidsguide@gmail.com

Additional copies
available at on-line bookstores

September 2018

Made in the USA
Middletown, DE
09 August 2021